MEDI CARE AGENT HAND BOOK

WRITTEN BY.
ALEJANDRO DUONG & ANH DUONG

LIBRARY OF CONGRESS
REGESTRATION NUMBER
XXXX-XXX-XXX
EFFECTIVE DATE OF REGISTRATION
MAY 17, 2023

MEDICARE
CLUB
INSURANCE

FIRST EDITION - 2024 / 13,508 WORDS / 160 PAGES
2024-V001-C002 - HEMINGWAY NATIVE - ARTIFICIAL PUBLISHING, LLC
COPYRIGHT ©2023, 2024 ALEJANDRO DUONG
COURTESY OF ARTIFICIAL PUBLISHING, LLC

TABLE OF CONTENTS

HOW TO STAND OUT FROM THE BORING INSURANCE COMPANIES

For Zelda

FORWARD

I spent much of my working life obsessing over the fact that I didn't need money. My brother once told me, "You don't want money, because you don't need it yet." I wish I had never heard that. I wish I never needed it. I earned my stripes as a writer, a musician, and a filmmaker. I tried my hands in marketing and was successful, but ultimately wasn't enough money. I realized marketing was only part of the solution. Now, I'd be lying to say my heart is in Medicare, that I love it. That would be a big lie. When my brother first introduced me to Medicare, I hated it. I didn't want to do it. I hated sales. I hated selling. I hated people. I never wanted to talk to another person ever again. That all changed when I started making money. I was good at it. I started learning. I started building my own style, my own strategy. I thought to myself, I can really make this work. One of the benefits that people don't know about selling Medicare, especially Medicare Advantage, is that we receive renewals, or residual money from our clients that have stayed with us through one (AEP) Annual Enrollment Period. So, if you have a calculator, now is the time to have it right next to you. As of this year, 2023, we get paid roughly $25 dollars per client, per deal, per month, until they either pass away or they cancel. The average telephonic agent does 4 deals a day. I only require 2 at my agency. At worst each agent writes 10 deals a week, 40 a month, at a 70% retention rate. So, if you are the very worst agent alive, you are holding on to 28 deals every month. We work roughly 11 months out of the year. That's 308 deals for the year. Let's say half of them fall off and don't make it passed AEP. Your gross revenue for your first year would be $46,200, and in the following year, which would be your second year, you would have a consistent renewal revenue of $3,850 every month without lifting a finger. The average member stays with

United HealthCare for 18 years, for example. Now, I have never been a wizard in mathematics, but I think you see my point. If you're in this game 3 years, you're set. The renewals compound, and if you do just as bad next year, the following year's renewals will probably be around $6,000 a month. Renewals hardly cancel. This is the value of being a Medicare agent and an expert in Medicare Advantage.

Now, in this Medicare Agent Handbook, I will give you the exact words to say on a call and it will be compliant for 2023. Next year we'll release the 2024 version to better assist you in your Medicare journey with the same value as the previous year. We double check everything and update this book throughout the year. You'll notice a serial number on page 3 that will let you know the version of this book. I will give you a call guide for every situation. I will give you lessons and tips, and statements that make your life easier on the phone. Follow the guide and you will have no issues. I leave you with my upmost appreciation for taking the time to read this, and I wish you great fortune in years to come.

Alejandro Duong

May 18, 2023

WHAT IS MEDICARE?

Medicare is a government-funded health insurance program in the United States. It provides coverage for eligible individuals who are aged 65 and older, as well as certain younger individuals with disabilities or specific health conditions. Medicare is administered by the Centers for Medicare & Medicaid Services (CMS) and is divided into several parts that cover different aspects of healthcare:

1. Medicare Part A (Hospital Insurance): This part helps cover inpatient hospital stays, skilled nursing facility care, hospice care, and some home healthcare services. Most people do not have to pay a premium for Part A if they or their spouse paid Medicare taxes while working.

2. Medicare Part B (Medical Insurance): Part B covers

medically necessary services such as doctor's visits, outpatient care, preventive services, durable medical equipment, and some home healthcare services. Part B requires payment of a monthly premium, which is determined based on income.

3. Medicare Part C (Medicare Advantage): Part C refers to private health insurance plans approved by Medicare. These plans, offered by private insurance companies, provide the same benefits as Parts A and B but may also include additional coverage like prescription drugs and dental or vision care.

4. Medicare Part D (Prescription Drug Coverage): Part D offers prescription drug coverage. It can be added to Original Medicare (Parts A and B) or included in Medicare Advantage plans.

Medicare provides essential healthcare coverage for millions of Americans, offering financial protection and access to medical services. It helps beneficiaries pay for healthcare costs, though there are typically deductibles, premiums, and copayments associated with the different parts of Medicare.

Original Medicare refers to the traditional government-provided healthcare coverage under Medicare. It consists of Medicare Part A (Hospital Insurance) and Part B (Medical Insurance).

While Original Medicare covers a significant portion of healthcare costs, it does not cover all expenses. That's where Medicare supplements, also known as Medigap plans, come into play. Medicare supplements are private insurance policies designed to supplement Original Medicare coverage by filling in the "gaps" in costs that beneficiaries would otherwise have to pay out of pocket.

Medicare supplements help cover expenses such as deductibles, coinsurance, and copayments that Original Medicare does not fully cover. These plans are standardized and labeled with letters, such as Plan A, Plan B, etc. Each plan offers a different set of coverage benefits, but the benefits for each plan are the same, regardless of the insurance company selling it.

To summarize, Original Medicare is the foundation of healthcare coverage provided by the government, consisting of Parts A and B. Medicare supplements, or Medigap plans, are optional private insurance policies that can be added to Original Medicare to help cover the out-of-pocket costs not covered by Medicare.

HOW TO BECOME AN AGENT

To become a health insurance agent, specifically a Medicare agent, you can follow these general steps:

1. Research and Understand Medicare: Start by familiarizing yourself with the Medicare program. Learn about the different parts of Medicare, eligibility requirements, coverage options, enrollment periods, and the overall structure of the program. This knowledge will serve as a foundation for your work as a Medicare agent.

2. Obtain the Required Licenses: Contact your state's insurance department to understand the licensing requirements for health insurance agents in your area. Most states require agents to hold an insurance license to sell health

insurance products. You will likely need to complete pre-licensing education courses consisting of 52 Hours and pass a state licensing exam consisting of 150 questions.

3. Get Educated and Certified: Consider pursuing additional education and certifications specific to Medicare. Organizations like the Centers for Medicare & Medicaid Services (CMS) offer training programs and certifications for agents, such as the Medicare Certification for Individual Agents. These certifications demonstrate your knowledge of Medicare rules, regulations, and plans.

4. Join an Insurance Agency or Brokerage: Look for opportunities to join an established insurance agency or brokerage that specializes in Medicare. Working under an experienced mentor can provide valuable guidance and support as you start your career as a Medicare agent. It also allows you to access resources, tools,

and potential client leads provided by the agency.

5. Build Relationships and Network: Networking is crucial in the insurance industry. Attend industry events, join professional associations, and actively engage with other professionals in the field. Building relationships with healthcare providers, community organizations, and local senior centers can also help you establish a referral network and generate leads.

6. Stay Informed and Updated: Medicare policies and regulations can change frequently. It's important to stay updated on the latest developments, new plan options, and any changes in Medicare guidelines. Continual learning and staying informed will help you provide accurate information to your clients and ensure compliance with industry standards.

7. Market Yourself and Generate Leads: Develop a marketing

strategy to promote your services as a Medicare agent. Create a professional online presence, including a website and social media profiles. Utilize various marketing channels, such as targeted advertising, direct mail campaigns, and community outreach, to reach potential clients and generate leads.

8. Provide Excellent Customer Service: Building a successful career as a Medicare agent requires providing exceptional customer service. Actively listen to your clients' needs, educate them on their Medicare options, and help them find the most suitable plans based on their individual circumstances. Building trust and maintaining strong relationships with your clients will lead to client referrals and long-term success.

Remember to comply with all applicable laws, regulations, and ethical standards while working as a health insurance agent. It's also advisable to consult with your state's insurance department and seek guidance from experienced professionals to ensure you meet all legal and professional requirements.

HOW TO SELL EFFECTIVLY

To effectively sell Medicare policies, specifically Medicare Advantage plans, consider the following strategies:

1. Know Your Audience: Understand the needs, preferences, and demographics of the Medicare-eligible population in your target market. Tailor your approach and communication style to resonate with them effectively.

2. Develop Product Knowledge: Gain in-depth knowledge about the Medicare Advantage plans you are offering. Understand the specific benefits, coverage options, costs, network providers, and any additional perks or value-added services. This knowledge will enable you to educate potential clients and address their questions and concerns.

3. Build Trust and Rapport: Establish trust with your clients by demonstrating your expertise, integrity, and commitment to their well-being. Act as a trusted advisor rather than simply a salesperson. Listen attentively to their needs, address their concerns, and provide personalized recommendations.

4. Effective Communication: Clearly and concisely communicate the advantages and benefits of Medicare Advantage plans. Use simple and jargon-free language to ensure that clients understand the features of the plans and how they meet their healthcare needs.

5. Provide Comparative Analysis: Compare Medicare Advantage plans with Original Medicare, highlighting the additional benefits and cost savings that Medicare Advantage offers. Emphasize the added value, such as prescription drug coverage, dental and vision benefits, fitness programs, and care coordination services.

6. Offer Personalized Solutions: Take the time to understand each client's unique healthcare needs, budget, and preferences. Offer customized solutions that align with their specific requirements. This could involve discussing plan options, explaining how certain features meet their needs, and helping them make informed decisions.

7. Utilize Technology and Tools: Leverage technology to streamline the sales process and enhance client experience. Use online tools, interactive presentations, and digital resources to provide real-time quotes, plan comparisons, and enrollment assistance.

8. Provide Ongoing Support: Offer post-enrollment support and assistance to your clients. Be readily available to address their questions, help with claims, and provide guidance throughout their coverage period. This ongoing support will strengthen client

relationships and potentially lead to referrals.

9. Stay Informed: Keep yourself updated with the latest developments, changes, and trends in the Medicare landscape. Regularly review plan updates, policy changes, and compliance requirements to ensure you provide accurate and up-to-date information to your clients.

10. Build Referral Networks: Establish connections with healthcare providers, senior centers, community organizations, and other professionals who serve the Medicare-eligible population. They can provide referrals and recommendations, expanding your reach and client base.

Remember to always comply with regulatory guidelines and ethical standards while selling Medicare policies. It's also essential to adhere to the training and compliance requirements set by the insurance carriers and regulatory bodies. Continuous professional development and staying informed will contribute to your success as a Medicare policy salesperson.

THE SEP GUIDE

Here are the details on the various Special Enrollment Periods (SEPs) available for Medicare enrollment:

1. Initial Enrollment Period (IEP): This is the initial period when you first become eligible for Medicare. It starts three months before your 65th birthday month and ends three months after. During this period, you can enroll in Medicare Part A and/or Part B.

2. General Enrollment Period (GEP): If you missed your IEP, you can enroll in Medicare during the General Enrollment Period, which runs from January 1 to March 31 each year. Coverage begins on July 1 of the same year. Late enrollment penalties may apply if you didn't enroll during your IEP.

3. Annual Enrollment Period (AEP): Also known as the Medicare Open Enrollment Period, the AEP occurs every year from October 15 to December 7. During this period, you can make changes to your Medicare Advantage or Part D prescription drug plans. Changes made during this period take effect on January 1 of the following year.

4. Medicare Advantage Open Enrollment Period (MA OEP): This enrollment period allows individuals who are already enrolled in a Medicare Advantage plan to make one change. It runs from January 1 to March 31. You can switch to a different Medicare Advantage plan or drop your Medicare Advantage plan and return to Original Medicare. You cannot use this period to switch from Original Medicare to a Medicare Advantage plan.

5. Special Enrollment Periods (SEPs): These are specific enrollment periods triggered by certain life events or

circumstances, allowing you to enroll or make changes outside of the standard enrollment periods. Some common SEPs include:

- Moving: If you move out of your plan's service area, you may qualify for an SEP to enroll in a new plan available in your new area.

- Losing Coverage: If you lose certain types of health coverage, such as employer-sponsored coverage or Medicaid, you may qualify for an SEP to enroll in Medicare.

- Dual Eligible: If you qualify for both Medicare and Medicaid (dual eligible), you have additional opportunities to enroll or make changes to your coverage throughout the year.

- Low-Income Subsidy (LIS): If you qualify for the Extra Help program, which assists with prescription drug costs, you have additional enrollment opportunities.

- Plan Non-Renewal: If your Medicare Advantage or Part D plan is not renewing its contract, you have an SEP to choose a new plan.

- 5-Star Special Enrollment Period: If you are enrolled in a Medicare Advantage plan or Part D plan with a 5-star rating, you can switch to a different 5-star plan once during the year.

It's important to note that specific eligibility criteria and documentation may be required to qualify for certain SEPs. It's recommended to contact Medicare or a licensed insurance agent for personalized guidance and assistance with your specific situation but seeing that you're reading the most awesome Medicare book around, I'll give you specific details directly from Medicare.

CMS ENROLLMENT PERIOD CODES & REASONS

NEW – I'm new to Medicare.

ICE – I already have Hospital (Part A) and recently signed up for Medical (Part B). I want to join a Medicare Advantage Plan.

RET – I'm new to Medicare, and I was notified about getting Medicare after my Part A and/or Part B coverage started.

MRD – I had Medicare prior to now, but I'm now turning 65.

OEP – Between 1/1 – 3/31: I'm in a Medicare Advantage Plan and want to make a change. Between 4/1-12/31: I'm in a Medicare Advantage Plan and have had Medicare for less than 3 months. I want to make a change.

MOV – I moved to a new address that's outside my current plan's service area, or I recently moved, and this plan is a new option for me.

RUS – I moved back to the U.S. after living outside the country.

INC – I was released from jail.

LAW – I recently got lawful presence status in the U.S.

LT2 – I live in a long-term care facility, like a nursing home or a rehabilitation hospital.

LTC – I recently moved out of a long-term care facility, like a nursing home or a rehabilitation hospital.

LEC – I left coverage from my employer or union (including COBRA coverage)

LCC – I lost other, non-Medicare drug coverage that's as good as Medicare drug coverage (creditable coverage), or my other, non-Medicare coverage changed and is no longer considered creditable.

EOC – I lost my coverage because my plan no longer covers the area that I live, or it ended its contract with Medicare.

MYT – I lost my coverage because Medicare ended its contract with my plan. I got a letter from Medicare saying I could join another plan.

PAC – I dropped my coverage in a PACE (Programs of All-Inclusive Care for the Elderly) Plan.

SNP – I lost my Special Needs Plan because I no longer have a condition required for that plan.

CSN – I want to join a Special Needs Plan that tailors its benefits to my chronic condition.

MDE – I have both Medicare and Medicaid (newly got Medicaid, my state helps pay for my Medicare premiums, or I get Extra Help paying my Medicare drug coverage.

MCD – I recently had a change in my Medicaid (newly got Medicaid, had a change in my level of Medicaid, or lost Medicaid.

NLS – I recently had a change in my Extra Help paying for my drug costs (newly got Extra Help, had a change in my level of Extra Help, or lost Extra Help).

DIF – I was enrolled in a plan by Medicare (or my state) and I want to choose a different plan.

PAP – I'm in a State Pharmaceutical Assistance Program, or I'm losing help from a State Pharmaceutical Assistance Program.

12G – I dropped a Medicare Supplement Insurance (Medigap) policy when I first joined a Medicare Advantage Plan. It's been less than 12 months since I left my Medigap policy. I want to switch to Original Medicare so I can go back to my Medigap policy, and I'm joining a Drug Plan (Part D).

DST – I was affected by an emergency or a major disaster (as declared by the Federal Emergency Management Agency, or by Federal, my state, or my local government.) One of the other statements on this page applied to me, but I was unable to make my request because of the disaster.

12J – I joined a Medicare Advantage Plan with drug coverage when I turned 65. It's been less than 12 months since I joined this plan. I want to switch to Original Medicare, and I'm joining a Drug Plan.

5ST – I am enrolling in a 5-star plan.

LPI – I'm in a plan that's had a star rating of less than 3 stars for the last 3 years. I want to join a plan with a star rating of 3 stars or higher.

REC – I'm in a plan that was recently taken over by the state because of financial issues. I want to switch to another plan.

OTH – Other.

N/A – Other explanation.

ACC – I requested Medicare information in an accessible format. I got less time to make my decision, or I didn't get it in time to make a choice before my enrollment period ended.

INV – I lost my Medicare Advantage Plan with drug coverage because I lost Medical (Part B) coverage. I want to join a Medicare drug plan.

IIP – I live in a long-term care facility, like a nursing home or a rehabilitation hospital. I dropped my Medicare Advantage Plan with drug coverage, and I want to join a Medicare drug plan. Plans are reminded to use election type code "T" for OEPI transactions.

OSD – I dropped my Cost Plan with drug coverage and switched to Original Medicare. I want to join a Medicare drug plan.

IND – I live in or (within the past 2 months) moved out of a long-term care facility, like a nursing home or a rehabilitation hospital. I want to join a Medicare drug plan.

IEP – I had Medicare before, but I'm now turning 65.

LESSON 1

STAY

ON

ACTIVE

**WE ARE HERE TO MAKE $$$$$
SO, WE WON'T HAVE TO WORK
IN OUR 50's. THIS IS YOUR BUSINESS
AND ONLY YOU CAN MAKE IT
SUCCESSFUL.**

HEALTH INSURANCE CALL GUIDE

IMPORTANT SECTIONS `XXXXXX`
CRM / DIALER RELEVENT `XXXXXX`
MUST SAY `XXXXXX`

**THIS IS A MEDICARE
PRESENTATION FLOW FOR
"TRAINING PURPOSES" ONLY: THIS
IS NOT A SCRIPT**

GENERAL INTRO

Hiii is this _____?

Hi, my name is_____with_____, and a Happy Monday by the way!?

Wonderful!

And thank you for being a member of Medicare. I'll do my very best to help you out today.

I'm actually calling because it looks like you may have requested some information regarding updated Medicare programs. Is that right?

Well, no worries, I've been assigned to help you out today, and go over all the amazing, updated benefits that you may qualify for.

[BUILD RAPPORT]

Great!

Now, your Medicare parts A and B are both active right? [MUST BE YES] Wonderful!!

If we get disconnected, is it okay to give you a call back on the number we have on file: phone number,

And your first name is spelled _____?
And last name spelled _____?
Just want to make sure we have the right person. LOL.

And what is your zip code _____? So, we can pull up all the new, updated programs in your   area?   Wonderful!

And this is your address, correct? Just need to verify it.[1]

[BUILD RAPPORT while you look up plans]

By the way, how is your day going?

[Choose one more additional RAPPORT talking point below]

How's the weather out there?
How's the family?

---

[1] Only ask this question if you already have their address. It puts them at ease that you have their info already and you're just verifying it. If you do not have their address, then code ahead move forward with that asking about it. You will get their accurate address later when you verify their MBI.

What did you used to do before you retired?

Now, do you understand all the options that Medicare has to offer like your Part A, B, & D, Plan F and G or does that get complicated like it does for everyone else?

Well not to worry. I am going to tell my supervisor that I am going to spend a little more time with you today. You and I are going to be a team. I'm going to help you out, okay?

And we don't have military insurance like TRICARE, right?

[MUST BE NO]

Great!

Are you still working or have any insurance from an old employer?

[MUST BE NO]

MEDICARE SUPPLEMENT INTRODUCTION

Ok Great, it looks like you do qualify for several programs in your area.

Now, are we relatively healthy right now? Are we suffering from any acute illness like diabetes?

Ms./Mr._____who is your current insurance plan with? Humana? Anthem? United Health Care?
Or do we currently have a supplement?

How much are we paying for that?

Is that a supplement? Or a Medicare Advantage plan?[2]

Are you trying to SAVE money by lowering the premium on your Medicare Supplement Plan?[3]

---

[2] If they have a supplement, then make it cheaper. If no, then you know we have to lead with MAPD.
[3] Only ask this if you think they have a supplement.

[IF YES][4]

[IF NO]

---

[4] Explain some of options briefly and calculate some estimations. If they are looking to get more comprehensive insurance. Continue through the Medsup process. If not and they want to save money, pitch the MAPD. Choose the right Medsup plan for them and follow the application per usual and read the summary of benefits for that plan. Remember med sups cover 20% that Medicare doesn't cover and all cost regarding Part A and b. You will need to sign them up for a PDP. Remember that can be with any carrier. If they want dental or cancer, there is an option depending on the plan. Read the benefits with those plans as well. No underwriting before 66, no smoking limitations before 70. ==Make sure they can afford the Medsup plan!==

MEDICARE ADVANTAGE CALL GUIDE

So, we'll stick with the lowest possible premium for your insurance and help you save some of that hard-earned cash! LOL

Speaking of which, how much do we usually draw from our social security benefits? Under a $1000 or over $1000 dollars per month?

Are you married?

[YES / WAS?]

Oh wow, you were married _____ years! What's your secret to a long marriage?

Wow! How much would you say you both draw in social security benefits monthly?

[NO/NEVER]

I'm not married myself. To be honest, I rather like the independence of it.

DISCLAIMER & SCOPE OF APPOINTMENT

Now, let me just go ahead and read a quick disclaimer before we start talking about some plans and getting some more info, just so we don't get in trouble from Medicare. Now, I was previously under the impression that you were interested in a supplement plan, but after speaking with you and learning a little bit about your situation, I think you might be more interested in learning about the new and updated Medicare health plans that are at no cost to you.

For your protection, I do need to inform you that this call may be monitored and recorded and maybe shared with insurance companies who administer the plans that we offer. I also want to let you know that you are not required to provide any health-related information unless it is necessary to determine enrollment eligibility.

Now, Mr./Ms._____we're just setting a phone appointment right now to discuss Medicare Advantage plans. Now,

Is it alright if we talk about your updated benefits you qualify for?

[MUST BE YES]

Awesome, now, my job is to help maximize your benefits today!

This is a Medicare Advantage plan. It takes part A (hospital benefits), part B (medical benefits) and part D (prescriptions) and combines them all to form what we call Part C - Medicare Advantage. Now you have a special election period, so it means that you are eligible to receive these benefits at absolutely no cost while still receiving all the benefits Parts A and B Original Medicare already gives you, plus more! Also, you will receive everything that we go over today in writing as well between 7-10 business days.

Great!

Go ahead and verify your date of birth for me please.

Mr./Ms._____? Thank you so much!

Wow you sound so young and amazing on the phone! What's your secret? I must know! LOL.

CHECK ELIGIBILITY

So, what I'll be doing next is see if you qualify for the new updated programs. As I mentioned, I'm here to help and to maximize all your options!

Now, Ms./Mr._____ do you happen to have your red, white and blue Medicare card available? That's the one that says Medicare Health Insurance at the top.

[NO]

Oh, did you misplace it? Oh, I see. There's another way we can look up your Medicare account. Go ahead and verify your social security number.

[NO]

Wonderful! Okay!

The only other way is authorization via date of birth.

Would you please authorize me to verify your Medicare information using your date of birth, and first and last name?

[NO]

Unfortunately, these are the only THREE ways we can verify your account.

Would you like my help today?

[NO]

Have a good day! [END THE CALL]

[YES]

Great, could you go ahead and grab your Medicare card for us also, please, and something write with, so you can jot down my number at the end of the call.

Please take your time. I'm here.

[NO]

If not we have to verify through either your social security number or your date of birth. We can't discuss a member's information NOT even with them, especially if they are not verified and give verbal authorization for us to access the information, for your protection, please!

[NO]

Have a good day!

[END THE CALL]

[MUST BE YES]

Perfect! Below your name on your card is your Medicare Beneficiary ID. It should be a combination of numbers and letters. Go ahead and read them to me slowly, please…

Wonderful! Give me one second. I'm just going to check to see if you qualify for the updated programs.

Let me verify your **MEDICARE number** again. Great! Okay I have your account completely verified. I see your Medicare Part A and B are both active on [DATE] _____. So that's great news!

By the way thank you for being a member of Medicare, once again. LOL.

[POA?]

Now, are we still making our own decisions regarding health insurance or does someone

Like a sister, a daughter, a friend?[5]

Wonderful!

When was the last time you saw a doctor?

Awesome, what's your doctor's name?[6]

Let me see if you currently qualify for LIS or Medicaid which can give you a little more. Always nice.

[Check if they have LIS or Medicaid]

Do you currently have Medicaid that you know of?

---

[5] *If they have a POA, try your best to guide them in a way that allows you to be that person for them and for you to help them because you are their new health care advocate. Technically POA's must be legal representatives.*

[6] Make sure that you also research the doctors address for later on the application. You won't be able to choose a plan, if you don't know who the doctor is. They may not be the type who'd like to change doctors, so save yourself the anguish and work on this as soon as possible, but don't talk yourself out of changing the doctor. If it needs to get done, then it is what it is.

[YES]

Great. I think I have your ==Medicaid number== here.[7]

[NO]

It doesn't look like you qualify for Medicaid, at the moment, but that's not stopping us. LOL. Let me see if we can at least qualify you for LIS.

[YES]

Great, it does look like you currently qualify for Medicaid or LIS. So, that'll help keep those prescription prices down.

[NO]

Ah, yeah it doesn't look like you qualify for that either. But that's alright. I have the perfect plan for you, let me go ahead and tell you all about it.

---

[7] You can pull Medicaid numbers in Vantage or Jarvis using the social security number.

CHOOSE A PLAN

I do have great news! It looks like you're fully qualified for a new, updated program with **[CARRIER]** and it is called the ***[PLAN NAME]***, and it's going to be $____a month, which is amazing.

It's an ***[HMO/PPO (DSNP)]*** with ***[CARRIER]***.

-**HMO** just means that your primary care physician will be able to help coordinate your benefits and refer you to a specialist in the network if you need to see one.

-**PPO** just means that you won't need your primary care physician's referral to go see a specialist. You can see whoever you want to, but keep in mind if they are out-of-network, you may have to pay more out-of-pocket. But you will have more flexibility, which is always a good thing.

-**DSNP** just means Dual Special Needs Plan. It's a plan for people like yourself who have both Medicare and Medicaid.

SUMMARY OF BENEFITS

When you see your primary care physician, it's a $____ copay.

A specialist visit will be $____.

Your plan does include preventative care services. Such as your annual wellness visits, flu shots, Covid 19 Testing and Vaccine. You'll have access to diabetes screenings, bone mass measurements, breast cancer screenings [IF FEMALE]. Prostate Cancer screenings [IF MALE], Physicals, and Lung cancer screenings. All at NO COST TO YOU.

God forbid, if you land in the ER, it would be $____ for days ____ to ____. If you had to stay a bit longer, days ____to ____ will be $0, so that is there just for your protection.

Next, let's go over medications.

[REVIEW DRUG COVERAGE].

[LIS 1, 2, 3, or 4 % or MEDICAID]

Because you have LIS or Medicaid, your medications *should* stay similar in price to what they are now. Tier 1 generic medications will always be $0. Then Tier 2 will be from $1.45 - $4.30. And last Tiers 3, 4, and 5 brand name prescriptions will be $4.15 - $10.35.

LIS 4 Your deductible is $104 and your coinsurance is 15% on all tiers until you reach your max-out-of-pocket $7,400. After that, it's $4.15 for Tier 1 and 2 generics and $10.35 for 3, 4, and 5 brand names and specialty drugs.

STANDARD DRUG COVERAGE

Are you familiar with the four stages of standard drug coverage? Medicare requires that we go over it, so please bear with me and keep in mind that you have this type of drug coverage right now. You will still have that moving forward.

Stage 1 is the Drug Deductible. This program has a deductible of $_____ which is amazing.

Stage 2 is Initial Coverage in which both the client and insurance company share medication costs until the shared total reaches $4,660. Depending on the plan, that can be shared through copays or coinsurance.

For a one-month supply of medications:

-Tier 1 preferred generics will be $_____
-Tier 2 generics are $_____
-Tier 3 preferred brands $_____
-Tier 4 non-preferred drugs $_____.
-Tier 5 specialty tier $_____.

Stage 3 is the Coverage Gap in which the client pays 25% of the cost of generics and brand names until you reach your max-out-of-pocket of $7,400 which includes deductibles, copays, and all coinsurances already paid in stages 1 and 2.

Stage 4 is Catastrophic Coverage, where the client pays $4.15 for generics, $10.35 for brand names, or 5% of the cost of drugs, whichever is greater.

[MUST ASK]

ARE THERE ANY MEDICATIONS YOU'D LIKE ME TO LOOK UP RIGHT NOW?

[SEARCH FORMULARY or GOOD RX]

Now, moving forward, this program covers your dental, vision, and hearing.

HEARING:

How's your hearing, by the way? If you need a hearing exam, it is $0. Great news! You get $_____ for hearing aids. Your copay for a hearing aids can be as low as $_____. They can be pricy, so you'll have help to cover the cost if you ever need that in future.

DENTAL:

In terms of dental, you actually will be paying $0 for all important preventative dental services such as exams, cleanings, and x-rays. On top of that, you also get a maximum benefit of $_____ to help you cover the cost of comprehensive services. That's your non-routine services like root canals, fillings, crowns, and dentures. So, you'll get that allowance to help with those costs, which is wonderful.

VISION:

When was the last time you got your eyes checked or got new glasses? It's always good to get an updated prescription to keep your eyes healthy. Now your eye exam will be $0 every year. You get a $_____benefit for your glasses, so make sure you get yourself a brand-new pair.

[61]

OTC:

Are you familiar with over-the-counter benefits and how they work? For example, when we go to Walmart or CVS to pick up items such as vitamins, Tylenol, bandages, etc...that stuff adds up quickly, doesn't it? So, this benefit is great because it helps you save money, but it also saves you a trip to the store. Moving forward, you get $_____ every (three) month(s) for your health and wellness products. You'll be getting a catalog in the mail, so you can pick up the phone, and order what you need. They ship it to you, and you don't even pay for shipping. Isn't that wonderful?

[Cover other benefits available on the plan depending on their needs: transportation flex card, healthy foods card, home health care, medical equipment, essential extras, meals, PERS, etc.]

FITNESS:

Last, your program includes a fitness benefit called Silver Sneakers! This one is more of a fun benefit. You can go down to a local gym or the YMCA and take fitness classes, work out, or just use the pool, hot tub, or sauna. You'll be able to take advantage of those facilities too.

CLOSE:

So, if you'd would like to take *advantage* of all these new benefits like the dental, vision and hearing, transportation, over the counter benefits which will help you save some money, personal emergency response system, so I know you'll always be safe and connected, don't forget the silver sneakers gym membership, healthy foods card, and all the other awesome things you're getting. All you have to do is wait till the first of the month. So on *[DATE]*, you can take advantage of all these wonderful new benefits!!! Ms./Mr._____, how does that sound at no cost to you?

[MUST SAY YES]

Fantastic! You'll love it.

[DOCTOR ASSIGNMENT]

Now, I just have to make sure your current doctor is in the system and actually takes this plan.[89]

(In-network)

Dr._____ is in the network which just means you can continue to go see your doctor for primary care. It's not going to cost you anything to see your doctor.

(Out-of-network)

In order to get you these new benefits, we need to assign a nice doctor for your care. Do you prefer male or female?

Fantastic. I also have their information pulled up if you would like to write it down. Otherwise, your (new) doctor's information will be on your new card as well.

---

[8] You should already have the doctor information in CRM and know whether the doctor takes the plan or not, so at this point you are preparing to decide whether it works, or you have to change the doctor to match the plan. Remember most complaints come from either changing the doctor or something with their prescriptions.
9

Are there any medications you'd like me to look up? Or any questions in general? Or should we move on to the last and final part [MUST ASK!!!]

Now, please write down *[PLAN NAME]* and *[PLAN PREMIUM]*, so you know it's not going to cost you anything starting *[DATE]*. We will send everything in writing to *[CONFIRM PHYSICAL ADDRESS / MAILING ADDRESS]*. It takes roughly two weeks to get your materials. Next month, you will show your new card: one card for everything including doctor, specialist, hospital, and pharmacy.

And just know moving forward I will be your AGENT OF RECORD or your Medicare Man or Woman. I'll reach out in a few weeks to make sure you got everything, and I just want to check in with you and make sure you're doing okay. We'll go over your paperwork if you like as well.

THE CLOSE

[REVIEW APP / CHECK SEP].

Now, Medicare does require that we complete your enrollment on a secure phone line. We're going to dial into *[CARRIER'S]* secure line, and you'll hear some terms and conditions for everything we went over today. It's a three-way call that has to be done in one go, so when there's a question, go ahead and answer with a YES, but don't worry, I'm going to be on the phone with you the entire time if you need help. I'll mostly do all the talking. Don't worry about the terms that do not apply to you. Once we get your confirmation number, we'll be done! *[READ or LISTEN to COMPLETE IVR]*

[GIVE CONFIRMATION NUMBER]

There are some health questions I need to ask you. This is so they know how to serve your area. Your answers don't impact your enrollment, and you can always decline to answer any questions *[COMPLETE HRA]*.

Mr./Ms._____, it was my pleasure. Your plan automatically renews on its own, and if you need to reach me, let me go ahead and give the

number to our Member Support Hotline
_____, and you can reach me there
no problem or if you have any burning questions
regarding your insurance and your paperwork.

I'll be helping you out moving forward, so don't
hesitate   to   call.

Also Mr./Ms._____, would you be interested in
getting a call back regarding a club membership
with us? It protects your Medicare information,
insurance programing, and offers a data
protection system from excessive phone calls
and spam and notifies us immediately of any
change in your insurance and we give you a call
back right away to fix it.

You currently have the Standard Plan with us,
which opens the Member Support Hotline to you
and Special Enrollment benefits all at NO
COST.

If you ARE interested in a little more protection
and customer service standards, spam blocker
and retention, then I can go ahead and make a
note here and someone from our Memberships
Team Department will go ahead and reach out
to   you.

Other than that, you're all set, Ms./Mr. ____!

LESSON 2

BE

LOUD

HALF THESE PEOPLE CAN'T HEAR. AND REALLY WHAT BEING LOUD IS ALL ABOUT, IT'S ABOUT BEING CONFIDENT AND COMMANDING. REMEMBER YOU'RE THE EXPERT.

REQUEST FOR NEW MEDICARE NUMBER

[ON A SEPARATE PHONE CALL]

[MINDSET] Clients must understand and know they need to change their Medicare number. Say this to the client.

Okay so Ms./Mr. _____, it looks like you've been switched from your plan. Have you given out your Medicare number over the phone? Have you been getting a lot of calls?

So, this is what we're going to do, we're going to call Medicare to request a new Medicare number because someone may have it and they're switching you without your consent. We just want to make sure that this doesn't happen again. This will prevent you from having any issues with medications or seeing your doctors and it only takes a few more minutes of your time.

So not to worry I will be with you the entire time and we'll request a new card from Medicare.

[Call Medicare - When on the phone with Medicare - Speak to an agent.]

Hi, I have _____ on the line and my name is _____ and happy _____ by the way. Mr./Ms _____ are you still with us? (Have the client say they are there)

So, I was talking with Ms./Mr. _____ and they have expressed that she's been getting harassing phone calls every day even on weekends, forcing her to read out her Medicare number over the phone.

They understand moving forward not to give out the number, but people keep calling and switching her their benefits without their knowledge. Isn't that right Ms./Mr.

_____

They keep calling you, isn't that, right?

We took care of their Anthem/Humana/WellCare/UHC benefits moving forward. For their protection, can we request a new Medicare number?

Can you help us with that today please?

ASK MEDICARE AGENT ON THE PHONE: Was the application submitted through Medicare.gov through another agent?

IF THEY HAVE A MEDICARE.GOV ACCOUNT: _____ Do you have a computer? Did you enroll in a Medicare.gov account? Is there an email associated? It'll be clients or POA's.

IF NO EMAIL: *Ask to deactivate account and change MBI. (Dr can't make changes with new card)*

AFTER HANGING UP WITH MEDICARE AGENT: *Tell clients to not give out their new card to anybody. Don't even give out your card to your doctor. You'll only use the updated Humana/Anthem/UHC/WellCare card we send you in 2 weeks.*

LESSON 3

SLOW

DOWN

THE MORE YOU SLOW DOWN, THE MORE THEY
GET COMFORTABLE. CLIENTS GET NERVOUS AND
THEY DON'T UNDERSTAND. THEY ARE EVEN
MORE NERVOUS WHEN YOU REPEAT YOURSELF.
YOU DO IT IN AWAY THAT MAKES THEM FEEL LIKE
YOU'RE NOT THE BEST PERSON FOR THE JOB. SO
JUST DON'T DO THAT AND SLOW DOWN, SLOW
DOWN, SLOW DOWN.

MEDICARE REBUTTALS

Medicare.gov Automated System: #, Speak to an agent.

Medicare Rep - If you can release the call?

Can Ms/Mr._____ do you give me permission to stay on the line to discuss your personal health information?

Will this replace my current plan?

Wonderful! You'll continue with your current plan from now until the end of the month. Your Anthem plan will start on the first of the month. You'll get all that Medicare Part A & Part B gives you plus more.

Yes, it will, how is your plan working out for you now?

I don't want to lose my Plan.

You will continue to use your current plan until the end of the month. Starting next month, the updated plan will begin.

I already have a Plan.

That is exactly why we are talking, there are always changes and updates to plans. I want to make sure you are taking advantage of all the updates in your area.

Will I get this in writing?

Wonderful! Yes, you will receive everything in writing between 7-10 business days. Does that answer your question? *(Verify Address)*

Decision Maker?

Does your son or daughter make your decisions for you, or do YOU make your own decisions?

Doctor NOT in Network

Looks like your doctor is not in the network but to help you with ALL these new wonderful benefits we just need to assign you to a doctor. Do you prefer a male or a female doctor?

Do I need to change my doctor?

Check to see if Doctor is in network early in the pitch if you feel like they truly wouldn't consider another Doctor.

Ask how long they've been seeing that, Doctor?

Ask how far they have to drive?

Based on their response most are open to changing for convenience and lower copays.

I already get all these benefits!

If you like the way your plan works now, you're going to love all these new wonderful benefits they've added for this year. I'll make sure to do all I can to help you out. (*Must have SOA)*

How long will this take?

This will only take a few moments and I'll be out of your hair.

Are you with Medicare?

I am a licensed agent, and I can look at the plans available in your area. I work with all the carriers in your area.

Will I still have my Medicare / Medicaid?

Yes, of course. In fact, you need them in order to even qualify for these plans. I want to make sure you are taking advantage of all the updates in your area.

BE THE TEACHER NOT THE SALESMAN

MEDICARE ADVANTAGE IS ALMOST ALWAYS AT NO COST TO THE MEMBER. SO, WHAT ARE YOU SELLING? THINK OF YOURSELF AS A GUIDE, AND YOUR JOB IS TO EDUCATE YOUR CLIENT. YOU NEED TO REMEMBER WE ARE ONLY HERE TO HELP AND WE SEE NO PERSONAL GAIN IN DOING SO. IT'S NOT ABOUT THE MONEY. IT'S ABOUT THE FACT THAT YOU'RE HELPING. BE EMPATHETIC.

<u>CHEAT CODES</u>

You can say this in any situation and be OK.

I'm here just to help you out. Would you like my help?

I'm here to help you go over all the new updated Medicare plans in your area.

Don't say SORRY. Say WONDERFUL!

Nothing will change. You're just going to get the extra benefits with your new updated plan.

Oh, that works. We actually work with ALL carriers.

Let me pull up your account and verify some information.

Medicare requires….

We don't want anyone else getting all these amazing benefits.

Do we make our own decisions?

That's a good question! Let me ask my supervisor. One moment.

You know, I don't know the answer to that, but I can find out for you.

Today is my first day, actually.

If it aint broke don't fix it.

I'll be with you the entire way.

This is the very last part before we get your confirmation number.

You'll receive everything in the mail between 7-10 business days.

You know, how Medicare is.

Everything will be zero dollars as long as you have your Medicaid active.

You're the boss!

Before I can even blink.

I'm your man. I'll take care of you!

Are you excited? / How exciting?

You have me now hon / dear!

You're part of my family, now!
Favorite color?

Who do I have the pleasure of speaking wth?

Wonderful! Beautiful! Fantastic! Perfect! Great!
Awesome!

You're in that lovely bunch.

Keep in mind..

I like that. You got a movie star name!

Your middle initial? What's that stand for?

No wonder we get along! We're born in the
same month!

So, you always have my information.

You're going to love this!

Later down the road.

It's like ordering a pizza!

The cherry on top is that you got me!

Do you want to grab some water, hon?
Let me know.

Let me go ahead and ask my supervisor real quick.

If you have any questions, you can always call our member support line.

Let me go ahead and ask agent support, give me one moment.

DON'T FORGET TO LAUGH

LAUGHING PUTS A MEMBER'S MIND AT EASE. IT LETS THEM KNOW YOU'RE EASY GOING AND HARMLESS. IT'S IMPORTANT FOR THEM TO FEEL COMFORTABLE, ESPECIALLY WHILE HANDLING THEIR SENSITIVE INFORMATION.

RENTENTION GUIDE

[USE THIS FOR MEMBERSHIP HOLDERS, CANCELS, SAVES, AND OVER ALL BLIND YEARLY CHECK UPS WITH CLIENTS]

Hi, is this _____? Hi, my name is _____ with the _____! Happy _____ by the way. I work with your Medicare Advocate _____! Does that ring a bell?

Wonderful!

I'm just giving you a courtesy call to say thank you for being a new _____ member. We helped you select your new plan for this year, so I just wanted to see if you got your new card in the mail yet?

[IF NO]

Don't worry, we'll make sure we send that out to you as soon as possible.

[IF YES]

Wonderful! I'm glad that you got it.

Now, I have your address / zip here as DOB
_____.

Oh wow _____you sound so young for your
age!

I also noticed that your benefits are ending this
month.

Are you aware of that?

Did you happen to talk to someone about your
Medicare benefits recently?

[IF NO]

Don't worry. What I will do is take care of that
today so you will have your updated_____
(carrier) benefits again for next month.

So let me go ahead and read you a disclaimer:

(ONLY IF IT'S MAPD)

SEE ORIGINAL CALL GUIDE or TRANSFER
THE CALL TO THE APPROPRIATE CALL
CENTER

LESSON 6

BE
EXCITED

YOU NEED TO BE HAPPY GENUINELY ABOUT ALL THE AMAZING GIFTS THEY'RE RECEIVING. IF YOU DON'T CARE, WHY SHOULD THEY?

THE FOLLOWING GUIDE IS AN EXAMPLE OF A MARKETING STRAGEY YOU CAN USE TO HELP RETAIN SOME OF YOUR CUSTOMERS. AS LONG AS EACH GIFT OFFERD IS LESS THAN $15, DOES NOT DISCRIMINATE, OR DOES NOT REQUIRE A MEMBER TO SIGN UP FOR A MEDICARE PLAN.

MEMBERSHIP GUIDE

Hi, is this _____? Hi, my name is _____ with the _____! Happy _____ by the way.

Wonderful!

The reason I'm calling is because it looks like you requested a call back regarding our Medicare Club membership?

It protects your Medicare information, insurance programing, and offers a data protection system from excessive phone calls and spam and notifies us immediately of any change in your insurance status and we give you a call back right away to fix it.

Now, you currently have the Standard Plan with us, which opens the Member Support Hotline to you and Special Enrollment benefits all at NO COST.

It pretty much stops scammers from calling, keeps your insurance on track, and offers you added benefits that work well with your current insurance.

Is this your address
_____?

And your phone number is
_____?

Wonderful!

I verified your account.

Would it be alright if we went ahead and talked about some of the additional benefits you can receive by being a member?

Is that something that interests you?

[NO]

LET THEM GO.

[YES]

KEEP GOING.

Wonderful!

Your current insurance plan is_____?

Is that right?

[NO]

VERIFY THAT THEY ARE STILL ON THAT PLAN AND/OR IF THEY ARE NOT ON THAT PLAN TRANSFER THE CALL TO THE ENROLLMENT DEPARTMENT AND MOVE FORWARD.

[YES]

THEN KEEP GOING.

So, let me go ahead and tell you about some options that may interest you.

The Standard Membership is $0 and offers our Member Support Hotline which gives direct access to dozens of Medicare Agents that can help you straight away.

It also includes access to all of Medicare's Special Enrollment periods that are sometimes unattainable to normal person over 65.

Since you already work with one of our partnered Medicare Advocates, you're current membership is at $0 which would normally be much more.

This is separate from your Medicare Insurance. This is a membership that helps individuals like yourself who have Medicare and who are worried about their information being hacked, insurance being switched, and scammers calling your phones.

Our team will take extra special care of you and make sure you always get a Christmas card from us.

Now, what I want to tell you about is our Classic Membership Plan.

Now, this plan is only $9 a month, and it's our next available plan that you qualify for.

Let me tell you why it's worth the money!

See, not only do you get the member support hotline and the Special Enrollment access throughout the whole year, but you also get much more.

These are some of the extra benefits you'll get.

- Plan Protection

- Data Protection System

- Scam Tracker

- Call Back Service

- Bonus Swag

- Membership Card

- Annual Gifts (For 1 Year Members)

Now, between you and me, my favorite part is the swag and gifts. They send out shirts, hats, pens, stationery, and even gift cards quarterly (every 3 months). Just to let you know how grateful we are that you're a member of the Medicare Club.

Now, the Plus Membership again, is only $9 a month and can be cancelled at any time.

How does all that sound to you?

Your personal information is in good hands.

[NO]

RESTATE THE BENFITS AGAIN AND OFFER TO ANSWER ANY OF THEIR QUESTIONS. IF IT'S STILL A NO, THEN LET THEM AND CALL THEM BACK IN 3 MONTHS.

[YES]

GET THEIR EMAIL AND OPEN AN MEMBERSHIP FOR THEM. TAKE THEIR CREDIT CARD INFORMATION AND SAVE IT ON THEIR ACCOUNT FILE UNDER BILLING.

LESSON 7

STAY
HEALTHY

AS MEDICARE AGENTS, WE TEND TO BE AT THE COMPUTER FOR MOST OF THE DAY. IT IS IMPORTANT TO TAKE FREQUENT SHORT BREAKS. DO PUSH UP'S, DRINK WATER, GO FOR A WALK. I CANNOT STRESS THIS ENOUGH. YOUR ATTITUDE WILL IMPORVE, YOUR FATIGUE WILL DIMINSH AND YOU WILL SELL MORE IF YOU TAKE THE TIME TO ADMIRE YOUR HARD WORK SO FAR.

GENERAL IVR GUIDE

This guide is intended to be used by a Licensed Agent who will be facilitating the enrollment process telephonically with the beneficiary or authorized representative enrolling on behalf of the beneficiary. All telephonic enrollments must be recorded, per Centers for Medicare & Medicaid Services (CMS).

The Licensed Agent must read aloud the Introduction, About the Plan, and Disclaimer sections (3) below; then read the plan section that applies to the plan the beneficiary or authorized representative is enrolling i.e., read For PDP Plans only if enrolling in a PDP plan. The Licensed Agent must read the Closing section verbatim while on the recorded call.

Introduction

I am acting on behalf of _____ and may be compensated based on _____ enrollment in a plan.

In addition, you understand and agree to this conversation being recorded.

Before we begin the enrollment process, I want to confirm that _____ understands that you will be submitting an application for enrollment into. At the end of this process, we will submit your enrollment request to the Centers for Medicare & Medicaid Services, known as CMS, for enrollment into the plan. CMS is the federal agency that runs the Medicare program.

Typically, you may enroll in a plan only during the annual enrollment period from. There are exceptions that may allow you to enroll in a Medicare Advantage plan outside of this period.

About The Plan

The program has a contract with the Federal government. will need to keep Medicare Parts A and B, and continue to pay your Part B premium. You can only be in one Medicare Advantage plan at a time. Enrollment in this plan will automatically end enrollment in another Medicare Advantage plan or prescription drug plan.

By joining this Medicare health plan, you acknowledge that this specific carrier will release information to Medicare and other plans as is necessary for treatment, payment and health care operations. You also acknowledge that this plan will release information to Medicare, who may release it for research and other purposes which follow all applicable Federal statutes and regulations. The information collected on this telephonic enrollment transaction is correct to the best of your knowledge. You understand that if you intentionally provide false information on this call, will be disenrolled from the plan.

For MA-only Plans

You understand that if you have Medicare prescription drug coverage, or creditable prescription drug coverage as good as Medicare's, you may have to pay a late enrollment penalty if you enroll in Medicare prescription drug coverage in the future.

For HMO Plans

You understand that on the date coverage begins, you must get all of health care from network providers, except for emergency or urgently-needed services or out-of-area dialysis services.

For PPO Plans

You understand that beginning on the date coverage begins, using services in network can cost less than using services out of network except for emergency or urgently needed services or out-of-area dialysis services. If medically necessary, the plan provides refunds for all covered benefits, even if you get services out of network.

For D-SNP Plans

This plan is a Dual Eligible Special Needs Plan (D-SNP). You understand your ability to enroll will be based on verification that you are entitled to both Medicare and medical assistance from a state plan under Medicaid.

For PDP Plans

You understand that if you don't have Medicare prescription drug coverage, or creditable prescription drug coverage as good as Medicare's, you may have to pay a late enrollment penalty if you enroll in Medicare prescription drug coverage in the future.

For Medicare Supplement & Ancillary Plans

Aetna is the brand name for insurance products issued by subsidiary insurance companies. The Medicare Supplement Insurance Plans are insured by Continental Life Insurance Company of Brentwood, Tennessee, American Continental Insurance Company, Aetna Health and Life Insurance Company, or Aetna Health

Insurance Company. Not connected with or endorsed by the U.S. Government or the Federal Medicare Program. The Medicare Supplement Insurance Plans are guaranteed renewable as long as the required premium is paid by the end of each grace period. The policies have exclusions, limitations, terms under which the policy may be continued in force or discontinued. Plans do not pay benefits for any service and supply of a type not covered by Medicare, including but not limited to dental care or treatment, eyeglasses and hearing aids. Premium rates are subject to change and may vary based on the effective date of coverage, and information provided by you. In some states, Medicare Supplement Insurance Plans are available to under age 65 individuals that are eligible for Medicare due to disability or ESRD (end stage renal disease). Plans not available in all states. Plan F is available only to those first eligible before 2020. Medicare Supplement rates based on issue age are valid only for enrollments with coverage starting before March 1, 2022.

Closing

Out-of-network/non-contracted providers are under no obligation to treat members, except in emergency situations. Please call Aetna Medicare's customer service number or see your Evidence of Coverage for more information, including the cost-sharing that applies to out-of-network services.

Services authorized by this plan and other services contained in your Evidence of Coverage document will be covered. Without authorization, neither Medicare nor this plan will pay for the services. You understand that your verbal attestation on this application means that you have heard and understand the contents of this application. It also confirms intent to enroll in the plan.

LESSON 8

BE

ORGANIZED

IT IS IMPORTANT FOR YOU TO HAVE A RECORD OF
EVERY SALE YOU MAKE AND TO HAVE AN
ACCURATE DETAILED CRM TO HOLD YOUR DATA.
A LOT OF TIMES IT TAKES THE WIND OUT OF YOU
BEING ON THE PHONE AND YOU FORGET TO KEEP
TRACK OF IMPORTANT DATA THROUGHOUT THE
PROCESS.

HRA GUIDE

Introduction

Have you served in the US Armed Forces?

Compared to others your age, how would you describe your health?

Do you have any acute illnesses such as COPD, Heart Illness, Diabetes, High Blood Pressure?

Prescription Drugs

How many different medications do you take each day (including prescriptions and over the counter medications)?

Hospital Stays

In the last year, how many times have you stayed overnight as a patient in the hospital?

Help At Home

On a scale of 0-10 how much physical pain have you experienced over the past 72 hours? Zero equals no pain and ten equals the worst pain possible.

Over the last two weeks, how often have you been bothered by little interest or pleasure in doing things?

Over the last two weeks, how often have you been feeling down, depressed or hopeless?

Other

In the past year, have you been unable to get any of the following when you really needed it? Food, Transportation, Clothing, etc.

Do you provide care for or look after someone who needs assistance with their care?

THIS IS

A

BUSINESS

**CONSIDER THIS A CAREER AND NOT A JOB.
DEPENDING ON YOUR CONTRACT YOU WILL BE
EXPOSED TO BUSINESS LIKE PRACTICES THAT
WILL HELP YOU IN YOUR FUTURE IN MEDICARE.
ONE TIP IS TO CREATE AN LLC, AS SOON AS
POSSIBLE, AND OPEN A BUSINESS-CHECKING
ACCOUNT TO SEPARATE YOUR PERSONAL FUNDS
FROM YOUR BUSINESS FUNDS.**

HOW TO GET FASTER

3 Minutes - Disclaimer and Scope
5 Minutes - Eligibility
8 Minutes - Choose A Plan
10 Minutes - Summary of Benefits + Close
30 Minutes - Enrollment
40 Minutes - IVR
45 Minutes - Say Goodbye

All Calls Should Be Under 45 Minutes.

They get tired and want to hang up the phone any longer than that. I used to have people fall asleep on the phone when I first started. I only took an hour, and they were checked out.

I had one lady that fell on the floor and pretended to be hurt just to get off the phone. It took so long. Seriously. I called 911.

It happens. The important fact you need to know is that these people are not wearing headsets. Half of them don't use a cell phone, and if the only house phone they own is the kitchen one with the long cord, then you're out of luck because you may have 35-40 minutes tops to say your peace. That's why I recommend that you stay under 45 minutes.

ASK THE

RIGHT

QUESTIONS

NOT YOU'RE NOT HERE TO SCAM. YOU'RE HERE TO HELP. BY ALL MEANS TAKE THE TIME TO MAKE SURE THEY UNDERSTAND AND THAT THEY WANT THE PLAN. MAKE SURE THEY SAY YES, NOT YEAH, NOT UH HUH, BUT YES.

COMPLAINTS

The below questions are what you will normally see on a complaints sheet from one of the larger carriers in the country. This is what they are looking for.

Did the agent clearly identify himself or herself as a licensed sales agent?

Did the agent ask for the beneficiary's name and determine if he/she is capable of making their own healthcare decisions?

Did the agent ask appropriate qualifying questions: 1) Entitlement to Medicare A and Medicare B ; 3) Existing coverage; and 4) LIS/Dual Eligibility (Extra Help)?

Did the agent secure a Scope of Appointment prior to beginning the presentation?

Did the agent conduct a proper suitability assessment to effectively identify needs and desires?

Did the agent clearly state the purpose of the presentation, including a description of the products to be discussed (e.g. Plan _____ HMO plan)?

Did the agent clearly state the purpose of the presentation, including a description of the products to be discussed (e.g. Plan _____ HMO plan)?

Did the agent conduct a proper suitability assessment to effectively identify needs and desires?

Did the agent conduct a proper suitability assessment to effectively identify needs and desires?

Did the agent clearly state the purpose of the presentation, including a description of the products to be discussed (e.g. Plan _____ HMO plan)?

Did the agent clearly state the purpose of the presentation, including a description of the products to be discussed (e.g. Plan _____ HMO plan)?

Did the agent determine and advise of the applicable enrollment/election period?

Did the agent distinguish between Medicare Advantage, Medicare Supplement, and Prescription Drug Plan products?

Did the agent follow compliant, ethical sales practices consistent with Humana expectations?

Agent must refrain from engaging in the following activity: 1) claiming to be endorsed by, or work for, Medicare; 2) providing vague guidance surrounding benefit coverage and/or broad generalizations in response to specific beneficiary inquiries (i.e. stating a MAPD covers what the 20% Medicare leaves behind); 3) engaging in high pressure tactics 4) providing false or incorrect statements about the plan; 5) engaging in cherry-picking.

Did agent thoroughly explain plan benefits (summary of benefits)?

Did the agent review the PCP and specialist network and how they work?

Did the agent confirm that the *prospect* wanted to enroll in the plan that was presented?

Did the agent state that the prospect will no longer be able to use their former health insurance (i.e., Original Medicare, Med Supp, etc.) after the effective date? insurance (i.e., Original Medicare, Med Supp, etc.) after the effective date?

Did the agent follow compliant process to obtain signature for enrollment including disclaimers?

Did the agent provide the proposed effective date?

Did the agent provide the following: 1) carrier name and customer service phone number; 2) TTY; and 3) application confirmation number?

Did the agent ask about alternative formats/other languages? (Ex: Spanish/French/Braille/Large Print/Audio).

LESSON 11

FOLLOW THE GUIDE

CMS IS PARTICULAR ABOUT WHAT YOU CAN AND CANNOT SAY. IF YOU HAVE EVER BEEN ON THE OTHER END OF A MEDICARE COMPLAINT THEN YOU KNOW WHAT I MEAN. "YOU CANNOT SAY FREE. YOU CANNOT SAY BEST. YOU CANNOT SAY, I THINK THIS IS THE BEST BECAUSE IT'S FREE. TRUST THE GUIDE. FOLLOW THE GUIDE. IT WORKS. STAY OUT OF TROUBLE. WE'RE IN THIS FOR A LONG TIME NOT A SHORT ONE.

__PERSON TYPES__

What are the 4 Personality Types?[10]

S- Structure
- This type of personality needs clarity and organization.

T- Technical
- This type of personality loves facts and solving problems.

A- Action Oriented
- This type of personality loves adrenaline, hitting goals and making history.

R- Relationships
- This type of personality loves

---

[10] Managerial resources or help in identifying personality types of clients – Important for the type of person they were before retiring.

people and being a
part of something
special.

Which Personality Type do you identify with?

S "STRUCTURE"

Of Paramount Importance to Me:

*Stability *Duty *Predictability
*Credentials
*Responsibility *Titles *Structure
*Dependability
*Belonging *Tradition *Rules
*Ownership

My Talents Include:

*Providing *Managing *Planning
*Organizing
*Preserving What Is *Logistics
Commitment
*Tenacity *Sequential Thinking
*Implementing *Responsibility
*Details

In My Starring Role:

- I expect everyone to follow the rules and regulations.
- I expect you to do what you say you will do.
- I set up & implement predictable systems.
- I trust proven authority.
- I tend to see the world in black and white.
- I accept a time-tested & proven establishment.
- I learn best through memorization, recall & drill.
- I run efficient meetings with an agenda & on time.
- I value roots & home.

- I dislike people who question authority or do not obey.
- I may insist on procedure for procedure's sake and not be responsive to need.
- I use the past to guide me into the future.

To Communicate with Me, Make A Big Production About:

- Concrete facts
- Details proven reliability and track record.
- Inclusion & belonging
- Predictability – I don't change easily.
- Being organized
- Increased efficiency
- Ownership which provides a sense of stability
- Punctuality

- Cooperation to reach organizational goals.
- Certainty
- Keeping commitments
- Low risk and safety
- Well thought out plans & systems

When I'm The Director (Leader), I Tend To:

- Be formal and I clearly define roles.
- Be demanding.
- Keep the organization on track.
- Focus on getting the right thing – in the right place – at the right time.
- Give specific details and relevant information to achieve specific results.

- Give feedback that focuses on getting back on course.
- Believe each person must earn appreciation.

And I Need:

- To be given authority before I will take charge.
- A planned, structures, stable environment
- To know the rules

When I'm Being Directed (Follower), I Tend To:

- Work better if the tasks & roles are defined well.
- Be responsible, diligent, and steady.
- Follow through with every detail.

- I carry out policies and procedures efficiently.
- Do things right the first time.
- Like leaders who have earned their titles over me

And I need:

- A sense of belonging
- Predictability
- Stability and security

I'm Sometimes Unaware:

- Of small contributions by people and my lack of feedback can be interpreted as criticism
- That in my quest for efficiency, I may seem callous.
- That I may focus on should and should

nots and not on
people's needs.
- That I can be too
cautious.
- That I take on ever-
increasing loads or
responsibility.

Areas I Need to Improve (Or Find a Supporting Cast to Help):

- I need patience with
others who work in
spurts and not at a
steady rate.
- I need to be more
open to change.
- I need to take more
risks.
- I need to hear
other's points of
view.
- I do care about
people's need to
overtly show that
care and concern.

T "TECHNICAL"

Of Paramount Importance to Me:

*Knowledge & Learning *Self-Mastery *Universal Truths *Insight *Competence *Concepts *Logical Consistency *Progress *Intelligence *Understanding *The Larger Picture *Accuracy

My Talents Include:

*Strategic Thinking *Dealing with Complexity *Rationality *Creating *Abstract Thinking *Theory Development *Problem Solving* Logic *Being Visionary * Perpetual Learning *Analysis *Designing *Using Precision in Thought & Language

*Searching For a Better Way

In My Starring Role:

- I trust logic & reason above all.
- I can map out a strategy overall plan.
- I am precise in my speech & notice contradictions.
- I desire willpower.
- I want power over nature & am attracted to science.
- I focus on long-term results & can project far into the future.
- I easily learn abstract ideas & can project far into the future.
- I can keep several issues in mind at the same time.
- I resolve conflicts logically, rationally,

and avoid emotionalism.

- I use diagrams & models to communicate abstractions.
- I am self-critical and usually spot my errors before anyone else.
- I dislike chit-chat & small talk and seek conversations with substance.

To Communicate with Me, Make A Big Production About:

- The rationale or logic behind an event or request
- Explaining the theory or principles behind an idea — the "why".
- An opportunity to learn — I must know.

- Getting to the point — efficiency of communication.
- Apologizing ahead of time when asking me to repeat myself.
- A method to change or improve something.
- The validity & logical proof of a new idea.
- New insights to solve a complex problem.
- Technical details & complexities.
- A person or object's genius, precision, and efficiency.
- Objective truth logical reasoning
- Consistency in the ideas presented, without excessive enthusiasm.
- Efficiency
- Ways to implement my ideas.

**When I'm The Director
(Leader), I Tend To:**

- Take charge, clarify the goal, and expect others to carry it through.
- Create a vision & build theoretical models.
- Look for talent & competence.
- Focus on efficiency.
- Be impatient with errors & inefficiencies.
- Prefer innovative projects.
- Work toward long term goals.

And I Need:

- To achieve a high standard.
- Complicated problems to solve.
- Relationships that work.

When I'm Being Directed (Follower), I Tend To:

- Want freedom to develop a strategy.
- Want the leader to be knowledgeable & competent.
- Sit & plan and not act if I fear failure.
- Design solutions to complex problems
- Be consumed by a project that's intellectually challenging.
- Avoid bureaucracy & time-wasting paperwork.

And I Need To:

- To have new ideas & approaches logically proven and validated.
- And environment to design or do

development without system hindrance.
- Time alone to reflect on a problem or idea.

I'm Sometimes Unaware:

- That I may be embarrassed by praise.
- That I offer solutions to problems others don't know they have.
- That I have little patience with people who don't deal in abstract thinking.
- I dislike repetition. I may be seen as terse or non-communicative.
- That I may be seen as critical and cold.

Areas I Need to Improve (Or Find a Supporting Cast to Help):

- Increase my ability to show praise to others.
- I need to recognize people's feelings — the human element.
- I need a team of people with a concrete and practical orientation.
- To keep me in touch with the here & now
- I may become so absorbed in learning that I don't act.
- Recognize the importance of logistics.

A "ACTION"

Of Paramount Importance to Me:

*Freedom Of
Action *Adaptability Spontaneity *
Action — Now
*Making An
Impact *Beauty *Stimulation
*Excitement
*Variety *Opportunity
*Options & Choices *Passion

My Talents Include:

*Promoting *Performing
*Entertaining
*Troubleshooting
*Tactics *Negotiating
*Improvising
*Handling Crisis
*Story Telling *Having Fun
*Competing *Flexibility
*Pulling Things Together
*Realistic Problem Solving

In My Starring Role:

- I am a skillful negotiator.
- I am an optimist and sometime proceed on blind faith (everything will be okay).
- I am graceful and have dexterity with tools. Baseball bats. And dancing shoes.
- I love beauty and the aesthetically pleasing.
- I recognize and go after opportunity.
- I try to find a better way to do it.
- I sometimes rebel against rules, routine, & structure
- I take risks to get things done.
- I am a natural entrepreneur.

- I learn best through hands-on methods– show me, don't tell me.
- I dislike boredom or waiting.
- I dislike abstract ideas & "useless" theory — get real!!

To Communicate with Me, Make A Big Production About:

- Freedom to act.
- The action involved.
- The bottom line first — and I'm always in a hurry, so talk quick!!!
- The chance to be the first, the biggest as you talk.
- The aesthetic beauty
- An opportunity.
- A chance to jump in & "show 'em how to do it."
- The variety of activities– with

minimal routine....no boredom.
- Concrete examples–not theories.
- How I can do it fast–probably faster than anyone else.
- A system in place to deal with things I dislike — paperwork, etc.
- Entertaining stories.
- Rewards & awards

When I'm The Director (Leader), I Tend To:

- Be pragmatic & do whatever it takes to get the job done.
- Exude confidence & expect others to obey.
- Be adaptable — if I find a better way, I'll change

- Not be governed by "the way it's always been done."
- Be resourceful.
- Find someone to do the "unexciting" tasks which are necessary for "a+" results.
- Motivate the team to "go for the gold.

And I Need:

- Problems to solve & a crisis to handle.
- Recognition for a job well done.
- Freedom to do it my way.

When I'm Being Directed (Follower), I Tend To:

- Challenge authority
- Ignore inconvenient policies & systems

if I can do it better or faster.
- Avoid confining situations.
- Thrive on action — I must be doing something.
- Trust my impulses
- Look for the immediate payoff.

And I Need:

- A leader who has earned the right to lead by a proven track record.
- To be shown the objective and given the flexibility to do it my way.
- A system to meet deadlines & finish projects.
-

I'm Sometimes Unaware:

- That I avoid making plans & commitments.

- That I get so absorbed in a specific activity and forget the long-range objective.
- That in my need for excitement, I may not see the dangers.
- That if I don't have a crisis, I may create one.
- That occasionally I need to stop … reflect … plan … get organized.

Areas I Need to Improve (Or Find a Supporting Cast to Help):

- Resolve conflict in a collaborative way.
- Make & keep commitments.
- Look beyond the quick fix.

- Take time to listen to other points of view.
- Recognize the importance of concepts and ideas (a solid foundation for my action)

R "RELATIONSHIP"

Of Paramount Importance to Me:

* Empathic Relationships *Identity *Significance *Harmony *Authenticity * Ideals *Involvement *Morality *Self-Actualization *Ethics *Cooperation *Personal Growth

My Talents Include:

*Diplomacy *Inspiring *Counseling *Using Metaphors *Empathy *Encouraging * Communication * Building Rapport *Imagining *Romance * People Skills * Mentoring

*Being A Catalyst * Envisioning the Ideal

In My Starring Role:

- I am potential oriented above all.
- I show appreciation easily — in many ways.
- I seek a deeper meaning than material possessions alone.
- I am enthusiastic and intense.
- I am on a quest for self- actualization and want to help others do the same.
- I learn best if the subject includes people… I need to relate to the teacher.
- I need people interaction.
- I dislike authentic or fake people.

- I am a supporter and confidant, empowering others to be their best.
- When change is considered, the #1 question is: what will it do for the people?
- In business, i stand out in recruiting, training, motivating, and counseling.
- I will discuss ideas, but if anger surfaces, I may leave.

To Communicate with Me, Make A Big Production About:

- Developing people's potential
- New ideas
- Involvement and cooperation
- The meaning of life and ideals
- The ethical

- A worthy cause — especially involving people or animals.
- Bringing out the best in myself or others
- How much you appreciate me and my efforts before any "constructive criticism "
- "The good "for both the people and the organization
- What you really mean (I can usually read between the lines for true meaning)
- Making an impact on people's lives
- Empowering
- Examples using metaphors.
- Building rapport & sharing personal examples

When I'm The Director (Leader), I Tend To:

- Make work meaningful for everyone, so it's more than a job.
- Foster a participative management style.
- Lead by coaching, empowering, & giving positive feedback
- Want systems that allow people to work together with minimal conflict.
- See associates as "real people ", not just number on a form.
- Focus on people's needs more than task demands.
- Try to help with co-worker's personal problems.

When I'm Being Directed (Follower), I Tend To:

- Like following an ethical leader who "cares ", rather than an authoritarian
- Resist changes that don't consider the people factor.
- Like collaborative teams
- Work to please
- Be more loyal to people than systems.
- Respond to warmth & kindness, not to cold rules & policies.

And I need:

- Appreciation, not criticism
- To be creative & still be with people.
- A higher purpose than day – to – day work.

I'm Sometimes Unaware:

- Of the negative, trying to find the good in even a bad situation, so I may get shocked by reality.
- That I personalize conflicts.
- That when learning, it's easy for me to see the big picture implications & miss the details (which may bore me)
- That I'm into people so much, I may neglect the goal.
- That I may prefer fantasy to reality and dreams to action.

Areas I Need to Improve (Or Find a Supportive Cast to Help):

- I need to be more assertive in conflicts.
- I ignore conflicts as long as possible.
- I must not get emotionally caught up in the problems or failures of everyone.
- I must encourage others to take responsibility.
- I must remember my own health & needs and not spend all my time helping others.

STOP SAYING UM

IF THIS IS YOUR FIRST TIME ON THE PHONES, IT'LL TAKE SOME TIME FOR YOU TO GET USED TO THIS. BE CLEAR AND SMOOTH. KNOW WHAT YOU ARE SAYING. "UM" JUST MEANS YOU'RE DOUBTING YOURELF AND YOU DON'T KNOW. IF YOU HAVE NO CONFIDENCE IN WHAT YOU'RE SAYING WHY SHOULD YOUR CLIENT? REMEMVBER YOU'RE THE EXPERT. YOU'RE THE ONE WHO STAYED UP ALL NIGHT STUDYING FOR THE LIFE AND HEALTH TEST. YOU GOT THIS!

Made in United States
Cleveland, OH
23 May 2025

17124727R00090